The Stanley Park Suite

BOOKS BY R. W. STEDINGH

Poetry

*Faces of Eve*
*From a Bell Tower*
*Faces of Eve* (Revised Edition)
*The Stanley Park Suite*

Translation

*Arved Viirlaid: Selected Poems*
(with T. E. Moks)

# THE STANLEY PARK SUITE

POEMS BY

# R. W. STEDINGH

LYRE Press
Vancouver
1999

LYRE Press
P. O. Box 88333
523 Main Street
Vancouver, B. C. V6A 4A6

Canadian Cataloguing in Publication Data

Stedingh, R. W., 1944-
    The Stanley Park Suite: Poems

ISBN 0-9685172-1-8

    I. Title.

PS8587.T424S72 1999   C8ll'.54   C99-901024-7
PR9199.3.S777.S72 1999

FOR MY MOTHER AND FATHER

## ACKNOWLEDGEMENTS

I would like to thank the editors of literary magazines in which some of these poems have appeared as follows:" Calla Lily," "Cherry Tree," "Salmonberry," "Coho Salmon" and "Rock Dove" in *The Capilano Review*; "Sleeping Polar Bear," "Arctic Wolf" and "Acrostic Numbers of the Killer Whale" in *Event*; "The Swan" in *PRISM international*; and "The Name of the Rose" in *The New Orphic Review*.

# CONTENTS

## I.

## II.  Flora

## II.  Fauna

I.

# THREE PRELUDES IN THE KEY OF GREEN

I.

Not in the hot beginning
But during the Ice Age,
Trees exploded, it got so cold,
And animals froze, rock-solid,
To the forest floor
As under the enormous
Weight of a glacier,
The land sank
Five hundred feet
Below sea level.

Then nothing germinated
Into nothing seen,
And the nothing seen
Became the nothing that remained
In darkness
Far under the blue light
Of ice and compacted snow.

Finally, in the Pleistocene,
The weather had a change of heart.
The ice retreated like a white snail
Back to the Arctic.
And as the earth's molten core revolted,
The crust shifted, tectonic plates
Crashed, the sea floor buckled

Upward, and as the land
Spoke its answer to the cold,
Out of the sea came this
Promontory rising
We call the emerald
In the city's crown.

II.

Today, still, what's left
Of the primal garden is a maze
Of unpeaceable kingdoms.

Most of the great trees have been slain.
Loggers with the heart of a beaver
Worked with a truck, dozer
A few cables and saws,
Dragged out the fallen
And sold their sound
Heartwood for money.

And what remains, still green,
Has been shaped by a mind
That loved formal gardens
Of paths, roads and shaven timber,
Hedges in a labyrinth,
Many elegant statues
And all the stones dragged
Off their glacial graves.

Still, the wild animals, like humans,

Die of each other,
And between plants and trees
The spider webs keep on shining.

III.

Here I come where it seems
All green is gathered to explode
Its song in the argument
Of light and shade;

Here I come to sing myself
As the landscape sings
Of green beasts, victorious vegetation
And stones that never die
Of inventing themselves.

Here is the ancient lyre
In a new day: plucked,
Plucked again and strummed,
Its music gives voice to those
Perfecting their childhoods
Into old age,

Which here is everywhere
Like a phoenix ever returning green
Into the being of itself.

# II. FLORA

# CALLA LILY

*(Zantedeshia aetheopica)*

*for Anne Burgi*

It may be Easter,
But your green is the spring day
In which all are resurrected,
The shy night in which bedded lovers,
Emboldened like acrobats,
Bring off their feats
Giving mutual smile.
You are the dew of my days,
Where the child in you leaps
Out of a winter grave.

But mark the heart-shaped patterns
Of this wild lily's leaves:
May we, out of such cloudy jade
Distil clear emerald,
Shape with closed eyes a seeing touch,
A hard, determined green
Of many facets, but of one light invincible
Through all the dark perduring
As music and song like this,
Which bodied forth
In the country of your love
Is yours.

# CHERRY TREE

*(Prunus avium)*

A soft memory of snow
Rising in your budding limbs
Flowers in the mirror of morning twilight.

You say nothing, flushed refusing,
As you root yourself deeper
Into the bluegrass blanket.

My lips, opening, kiss your flowers
Like an ocean breeze,
And the womb of your branches throbs:

Hereafter, feelings,
Shall we speak volumes in eyes,
In silence, our common tongue.

# SALMONBERRY

*(Rubus spectabilis)*

Reaching through thorns,
I pinch your pink nipples firm
Between stung fingers,
And the whole of you quakes.
I take you into my mouth
Till my tongue bleeds
Or you bleed. The taste is
The same: sweet, with an edge.

# RED CEDAR TREE ON THE CLIFF EDGE

*(Thuja plicata)*


Green fountain reaching for the light,
Your roots are hooked into
Any crack they can find, into
The earth's darkness. Drawn on
By a gravity that pulls them down
With promises of water and rich soil,
Your roots break from the cliff face
And dance, rooted in nothing but air.

Growing inside, your rings are echoes
Of darkness and light in the weather
Which turn your bark red as a scab.

But flocks of light
Graze on your green fire,
And the sun travels
To come back to you
Who are a red pillar
In a green cathedral.

Like a continuously burning bush,
Born of its own ashes,
Its own dead leaves and fallen branches,
Nothing stops you and you stop at nothing:
In spite of torrential rains, wind and snow,
You grow, stretch, crack and do not fall.

# FRUIT OF THE DOGWOOD

*(Cornus florida)*

You

      The dogwood berries
      In a ray of light

            Swell into red
            On the branch

Like drops of ritual blood
For the songbirds to swallow

# CROCUS

*(Crocus susianus)*


Your green shoots riot
                    Burst
Through the surface of the earth

                    Holding the snow
                    Raising it high

Overhead
        Like a weight-lifter

By strength alone
Spreading warm
                The rumour of spring
                        In the frozen flower beds
At our stamping feet

# SALAL IN SNOW

*(Gaultheria shallon)*

Your heart-shaped
        Lacquered leaves
                Breathe
Sunlight
    Reflect its milky white
        And never close or fall
Like your evergreen eyes
Before my face
        Even in dark rain
        Even in snow

# RHODODENDRON

*(Rhododendron macrophyllum)*


Full-breasted rhododendron,
You open your pink blouse
For the hands that first pressed
Your roots into the earth.

# SWORD FERN

*(Polystichum munitum)*

Lower life form,
Even among the true plants,
How you reach high
Your being
Above the deaths
Of the fallen leaves.

Your fronds like a fist
Full of swords burst from the dark
At the centre of light
Finding faint rays that filtre down
Through the canopy
Seeking anything green
So close to the earth.

Although you are lower
Than the understorey,
I read your primitive innocence
As it covers the open
Forest floor,
Uniting the spaces
Between the trees.

# SKUNK CABBAGE

*(Lysichitum americanum)*


Growing out of the swamp,
Your green spadix erects
Itself from the yellow spathe
Like the happy sex
Of a green woman,
Your fetid perfume,
A sweet excitement
To my growing nose.

## TULIP

*(Tulipa gesneriana)*


Your red bud
                On its thick green stem
                                Rises
Into the warm thighs of air

And blooms
                Briefly

Until your petals spill
                    In the wind

And you remain a green
                    Androgynous light

# THE NAME OF THE ROSE

I.

Star dust refined and stirred. Hybrid
Seed. Essence sculpted into abundance
Like a red statue in the gardener's hands,
You are an endless chore of fertilizing
With bone meal and manure, watering,
Weeding around, a careful cutting
Of the buds of audience
So the central bloom of summer
Might overflow.

In autumn, you are the mindful pruning
Of thorny stems, the mounding of earth
And dead leaves around your stocks
That will keep you warm
Throughout winter.

In spring, after you lance the earth
With the barbed swords of new shoots
And find leaf, chemicals are sprayed like lies
About your green stem and bud.
But all insects home to your fragrance
Like errant knights: pale green aphids,
Whole armies of them, turn black and die,
And drunken beetles dive past your red edges
To disappear in hunger's orgy, tearing
Till sated and gloating, they dip in flight

Heavy with your treasure and your poison.

To all this labour your high breed yawns
As if in the air of elsewhen, ancestry unknown,
Yet evolved, into this red delicacy
It is agreed is love.

II.

Deaths never seemed to die like this,
Nor love seem ever so unrequited,
But journeys taken begin and end in you
Like dreams of sleep undreamt at waking.

*Tabula rasa* waiting for the pen to write
And write on, you are all metaphor,
The elements forming like petals in the mind.
Yet in tight bud, shaped like a green tear,
You fall for no one.

Unseen light charmed from the unseen,
The black matter or darkness forming your
        centre,
Your green calyx peels back like a star
Revealing a red giant that explodes
To form again a black singularity
Swallowing whole stars till sated
It evolves, a universe
Blooming farther than human vision.

Thus, you become an exercise in hope,

Intricacy chipped, charmed into elegance,
A natural faith, a red fountain of charity
Whose petals caressing memory as outer light
Loosen one by one and spread
Drinking from their centre the infusing song
Like a solar storm at its height,
The androgynous, molten core.

III.

Logs collapse under the weight of a flame;
A flame, under its own weight,
And clearly you are a circle of flames,
The pure heart of the garden, like a cross,
A four-petalled rose, like an "X,"
Inexorable as zero.

Rose of fire, you grew black in Egypt,
Or so your history goes, and disappeared,
Returning everywhere among men, wild,
        innocent,
Yet to the false immune, your red crown
Stemming from one light,
Itself a turning thread, a circling skein,
Like the earth which frays and vanishes
With the horizon at night.

Or like the brain on its stem,
You are a flaming hive
Where the mind is a halo, a red aurora,
A round cluster of thoughts

Crazed as bees about their queen.

How like the atom you grow, a carpel surrounded
By anthers, both surrounded by red petals;
A charged centre in balance
With circling electrons;
How like the flight of the charmed quark,
Its helix of disappearance into itself;
How like you flowering into absence,
A stirred presence ever-changing,
A flame that dies to live and lives to die.

IV.

All night, mist cooling
Falls to it knees
And clings to the red edges of your petals
Till it wells up in pools on your surfaces,
Embracing your pollen and dry perfume
Till it trickles, a spring of diamonds,
Gems of the dark's inner light,
And my rose-tongue talking rose
To you is gold with the carpels
Emerging from the lips of your corolla,
The unfettered heart of you rising to touch,
A deep song being entered and sung
By a shaft of light in the sudden afternoon:
Your petals against petals press argument
Like an urgent mouth honeyed
After the first sweet kiss.

And yet, you are wise enough
To be nothing but yourself
And caress yourself aglow
To find in space your own image
In a man.

Like an eyelid closing, curling upon itself
So tightly to prevent the light's androgyny,
You subdue both inner and outer sight,
Keeping darkness within, distilling it
Until your petals are engorged with blood,
And you throb again
Condensed as a cloud in red twilight
Raining nectar and sweet attar.

V.

Stocks and stems strung out like barbed wire,
A rutting bramble of green above which you
    grow,
And with which I contend, incontinent,
It is still your green dark that I love,
A new place of perpetual surprise
Where blood blooms in wounds of flesh
And is everywhere stifled into season
Like a song that lives of constraints
And dies of freedom.

Brimming with being
And bending into the wind, you offer
Yourself like a fulcrum

Of the unnameable God,
In silence pronouncing the unknown name.

Never able to give of yourself
But yourself, you are a gyring presence
With great spaces
To fill emptiness as well,
For all around you and because of you,
The garden is lost:
Trees hide in their shadows throughout the park,
The traffic races and stalls just beyond you
On an asphalt road as slick as an eel:

All are diminished, for nothing
But inwardness blossoming triumphs
Like a dormant anther aroused
And splitting open as it curls
Under the faint web and distant gravity,
The influence of dying stars.

VI.

Sweet attar, a mirror of floating
Tea leaves and temple incense
During a study of the fire sermon,
The broken women want to wear you
As talisman and lure,
As healing air,
To bring back the swagger
Of intoxicating light.

## VII.

You continue to spin your petals
Around green carpels and golden anthers,
And in a tight sheath love is fused.

There, only tender touches fill you
With hesitant happiness
Which between two lovers thrives
As it was at the beginning,
And rarely, even now.
Each rendez-vous with the wind
Is a new marvel blooming
In longing eyes
To flush the face.

Every day you are a heart struck
By the sudden brilliance of the sun.

## VIII.

In cross-section, rose,
You are curved like the turtle shell butt
And arching antlers about the strings
Of the lyre, which is nothing without love.
Plucked by the plectrum
In left hand or right,
Your ancient silence
Before timed number,
Before speech,
Nods in a gust of wind

And spills its petals
Over an abundance of roots
In firm ground,
A silent centre
Itself singing
All mandalas, all fractals
Like the still point of the pirouette
When the dancer spins into the dance.

# MEDITATIONS ON A BLADE OF GRASS

*(Graminea agropyron)*


Your emerald sword extends sunward

From innocent roots

Drawn to the centre

Of the earth

Between tropisms

Your answer to the weather

A perpetual erection

Like the clitoris

Of a green woman

That unites

Earth and sky

*

Carbon dioxide, water, starch and light:
Your chlorophyll, a green matter

That inspires, expires—
A breathing
Poem.

*

Stepped on, you bend
Till the weight passes.
And spring up
Verdant in every season.
It is the only colour you know.

*

Your sunward surface smooth;
Your shaded side rough:
I tug at you between forefinger
And thumb. You tug back
With all your might
And make a squeaking sound.

*

Mown. Your head hacked off,
You think with your roots
Reaching underground
And only grow higher.

*

39

You are one string
Of the earth-lyre,
Which is all living things.
Plucked by the wind,
You hum and vibrate
An enormous music
Of immortal green.

*

Always
The smell of you
Is sweet in the air.

*

I pluck you from the lawn,
Chew on you like a sick dog
Hoping you'll make me well,
But your taste is bitter
As the end of all that is green.

# CANADIAN THISTLE

*(Cirsium arvense)*

Your purple passion
Is poised
On the end of your stem
Like a flag wanting patriots,
But your leaves
Tell the tale
With their crown of thorns
Pointing outward
From the edges
At any passer-by.

# III.  FAUNA

# ROCK DOVE

*(Columba livia)*

Shy as you are, and non-committal,
You do not see this woman's open hand
But the empty palm,
And in challenged doubt, a weapon,
And you peck it
Before it pecks you.

A fist, too, is worthless,
Though blunt to you,
Till it opens proffering popcorn:
Then you are all courage,
By hunger blinded, by her indolence
Controlled.

Teasing the exploded seed,
Which will never know its own careful flowering,
You dance in nervous circles,
Weaving near and far,
Shredding the white heart on the pavement
Till a delighted child chases you away.

# PEACOCK

*(Pavo crestatus)*

The chameleon of cold in your blood
Climbs up your spine: you turn rigid
And strut, transformed,
A diamond, colour-armed,
Your splayed toes finding
The earth too small,
Your tail, a green forest
Crowned with golden suns
Like eyes staring out,
Staring in,
Grave in their own gravity:
The mountains of the moon
Are never so plumed.

From the deep blue of your head
To the green and gold shingling of your body,
Your feathers yearn still to touch the light
Beyond your strut and stride
As you stare into the central eye,
The soul of the moving yet unmoved.

Looking out of your own dark stare,
You fix me, but see no other beyond yourself
As if to say, "You are not here;
Nor is anyone else." But you are
A cry painted silent. There is no other

That continues the scream
Like your glare and shriek of terror
Whose stiff posture would complement,
As statuary, the contorted dead.

Even now, out of the jewels
Of your plumage, you bare your heart,
The core of your mind,
And your cry out-cries and crashes
Among the branches, the blades
Of great leaves, the seeds and rinds
Of rotting fruit and green thickets of light,
Deeper than shadows, the emerald sheen
Of your body out-shining,
Lending moment to all that is green,
Your scream both a clarion
That no dark is
And a herald of sudden fright.

Thus, morning finds you, as the evening,
In high places, like a medieval courtier,
Roosting on roof-tops or in tree-tops
To catch up there the sun's first and last rays,
For it is you who wait in the cold
For the air to warm where night had been.

# MORNING RAVEN

*(Corvus corax)*

You leap out of a cherry tree
After the rain,
And for hours I hear you
Gargling the wet morning
In your throat
As large drops well up in the leaves.
Then you spiral like black snow
Onto the lawn, pretending to melt there
Where you sparkle in the sun,
Your darkness taking on the colours
Of the light: you are
A black prism, your feathers
Iridescent as you pace
To and fro, fro and to,
Waiting for the dove
And the green earth to begin.

# BLUE HERON

*(Ardea herodias)*

A wild patience, hunger-honed,
A mind wrapping the body like a cloak,
You stand desolate as driftwood,
Neck cocked and still as a branch,
Waiting for the first fish to shine
In shallows at the tidal edge.

*

Below the false surface of the water
With its calm and reflective light,
You see something glimmer in the moon's tide
And stab through your own image with your bill
A sliver of silver light
That flashes its electric tail
Down the full length of your throat.

*

A crow swoops down at your head.
You spread your wings wide,
Baring your heart,
Even under attack.

## THE SWAN

*(Cygnus olor)*

I.

All grace in air comes to water
In the rhythmic lunge of the neck;
The wings out, white, tighten,
Like the song you sing in air,
A huge silence moving.

Then gravity turns you in one direction
On your own image:
In a gliding hiss of water
You wear all mirrors,
A wet world that slows you down,
Insular, to preen a heavy grace

Like hard light in drift ice,
A lasting blue.

II.

A proud face burning
Red with reprise;
A head like no one's,
White, even in disguise.

Yet you seduce yourself

With glances in a calm:

The barbed bill spoons,
Your neck becomes a snake,
And the water speaks
Like shattered glass.

III.

Competition is a presence
On the broken water.
It arrives like one's self,
As graceful as the wind,
As threatening: it bares
The eye to dark and light within.

The only weapon is a feather,
The only shield a wing
Arched like a cage over the back.
Then there is always the beak.

IV.

You put your foot down
And feel the earth move
In twilight like a tide, shifting
And heaving under you
Till you seize in the eyes of a woman
Starlight you never dreamed of
And the sudden shape of your love,
The equal of terror, which leaves

51

In its track a web of gurgling silence,
A heart of precious stone.

V.

Finally, you turn, like a white galleon
Launched on what remains
Of the ancient flood,
A bird of endless departures
Who runs on water
Into the air again
Where you disappear like an allotrope
Of alpine snow
Far beyond what a man can see.

# SEAGULL

*(Larus glaucescens)*


Even in a group you are solitary,
Nipping at the ankles of your brethren,
Keeping them at bay and momentarily lost,
On edge, in your great distance.

Perched white on the earth
Which seems too small
A place for your webbed feet,
You are a silent waiting waiting
For the picnickers to turn their faces
From what they are eating.

Then you swoop down, a great devouring
That steals the food poised at their lips.
And they curse you in their shock,
Forever after guard their food,
And you are never trusted, but remembered
As a wild thing, no longer common or domestic,
That takes his hunger everywhere
In a ferocious, yellow beak
That does not stay to be touched.
You are always on guard against
Such nearness, such pain,
And your solitude grows larger, hungrier,
With a hunger that feeds
On its own hungriness.

# A RACCOON KNOWING BETTER

*(Procyon lotor)*

Little nimble feet combing
The shores of Lost Lagoon
For frogs and garbage.
Only for a moment are you
Left alone by the crowd of people
Content to admire your ringed tail
And the black eyes in the mask
Of your face as you eke out a thin existence
Where shadows cluster around the light
Of a sultry August afternoon.

But you are left alone no more
As the people try to feed you as you hunt
In what's left of day. They toss you
Popcorn, peanuts, crusts of bread
And whatever junk food they eat
In an effort to come close and pet you.

You climb a tree to be safe,
Beyond their reach
To tame you.

# LESSON OF THE CORMORANT

*(Phalacrocorax penicillatus)*


You are, in fact, a flying stomach
Which, inside-out, is the sea;
You are a chimerical flag
Furled on a rock, wings out to cool
And waving green in sudden sunlight,
Black again under the clouds.

Aloft, you dive into your own
Diving image into the emerald waters
Of the Narrows, flying under water,
A nightmare that scatters schools of oolichan
Like skeins of light. They believe
Their freedom is to go anywhere
In their collected shape,
The form of an unthrown net
With no net anywhere in sight.
Banking this way and that,
They collect into a communal fear,
A cloud you dart through open-mouthed
Filling your crop
With their schooled selves.
But what they have learned,
They have learned too late.

And you fly back to your nest
High on the cliff-face,

Regurgitating into the open
Beaks of your young
What you have found
In the real world.

# CANADA GOOSE

*(Branta canadensis)*


Flying saxaphone
Or waddling bagpipe,
You are always solo
And improvising
As you navigate
The rhythmic quiet
Of the flock
Already on the ground.

Honking in tongues, at intervals,
Your staccato voice
Punctuates the gaggle with a plea
That goes unheard
Until you find yourself
Extemporizing your life
For naught but madness
In solitary song.
It is then they run
From your head
And neck charging low
Over the ground
And gone suddenly reptilian
As you hiss and spit out
Your territory.

Or

Finding none,
You leap into
Your reaching wings again,
Till at a certain height in the blue,
You realize you have lost
Your way to the moon.

# SNAPSHOT OF A MALLARD DRAKE

*(Anas platyrhynchos)*


You moult all that colour
                Greens blues and yellows
Become remarkably tame
                Taking on the plumage
Of a dull brown female
                Just to mate

# AFTERNOON OF THE WILD SQUIRREL

*(Sciurus carolinensis)*


I strike two stones together like cymbals
    Click
        Click
            Click
And you run in your greyness
    Down your tree trunk
    Through the understorey
    Across the sidewalk
    To the bench where I sit
And climbing up my pant-leg
    You sit in my lap
        Begging
            For peanuts
As if you knew me
    Who
        A creature to run from
Seems to be tame

# COHO SALMON

*(Oncorhynchus kisutch)*

I.

Always, it seems, Love, even in sleep,
Your silver hips wave, flash and flutter
Like leafage in the wind
As you crowd the mouth of the Capilano,
Tail sweeping back and forth
Against the darkness, against the light,
Swimming deeper and deeper upstream
Into less and less
The higher you go
Into the unseen mountains.

II.

While all is done between us, you continue,
Love, the journey:
Beached on a rounded stone, you flap
Against earth like a red moon
And fall, till gills flared,
Your eyes before my eyes clouding,
As your lips open and close
Trying to say something entering death,
Surprised to see me standing here
And breathing air.

# SEA URCHIN

*(Strongylocentrotus drobachiensis)*

High tide and sea wave
Toss you into a furrow
Of shifting beach sand.

But your green spines like antennae
Find anchor in what moves
You, and you bask like a bather
In the lips of the sun

Until a crow seizing you bears you aloft
Over the rocks. Though the height makes you
Dizzy, you hide your heart,
Like a thistle, and it is difficult
To say whether you fall into yourself
Or the feathered dark lets you go.

As you plummet, you remember yours
Is a green generation, hard as an emerald,
That you are not lost, clinging to yourself,
And you bounce off the rocks
Back into the sea.

# IV.  ZOO STORY

# MULE DEER

*(Odocoileus hemionus)*

In a fenced clearing
Of the wooded park,
You bow your head
To graze at the edge of a puddle,
Cleft hooves locked in every quadrant
As you dwell in the open,
Concealed no longer,
An ungulate ruminating.

But even in this green pasture
You worry, as if still
In the wild, at twig-snap
And leaf-rustle, and you stop
Chewing the cud, to raise
The great bone lyre of head and horns:
The air is gored into
A jagged silence,
The grounding of words.

And your ears straining to hear
Dart to the rear, pan forward
And back again as the miniature train
Full of cheering children
Blows its high whistle in passing.

Between green shadows of forest

And grass, reflected light
From the water quivers
On your upturned throat
As you snort into the wind
And bray the song of your disdain
At the retreating train.

# SLEEPING POLAR BEAR

*(Ursus maritimus)*


Your eyes twitch under their lids
In a place of chasing,
Where the whimper of you seems gentle,
Rings out terrible, running after seals.
There, the ice cap is licking like a torch,
Full of running, laced odors,
Bones stalking, and leaps into
So little that is tamed, yet so much
That people would find deeply familiar there.
And you are still there often, even in the caged
    grotto,
Your very eyes the unfathomable knowledge
    behind
Your face, the mystery of your will, appraising
Such carnage and triumph, standing there
Strange even to yourself the moment you wake.

# BLACK KING SNAKE

*(Lampropeltis getulus)*

Imprisoned king,
Now you can see through
The walls of your empire
That you are trapped.

Though you shed your skin
And emerge like a black resurrection,
You rise falling every time
Into a smaller contortion.

Coiled like an endless rope
Upon itself, you fester
Under the incandescent bulb
Lighting up the fact that you are

Indeed here, and many times longer
Than the glass cage in which
Only your tongue darts out
Like a candle flame

Shedding light only on
The immense length
Of your existence being never
Able to unwind.

# BIGHORN RAM

*(Orvis canadensis)*


All year your mind zeroes-in
On its only season, the time of ewes
In heat calling out
From the oestrus of the heart,
And you are consumed
By the rut you would consummate.

And here in the fenced yard
Among grey rocks, green tufts
And spindly thickets on the uneven
Ground, you stand under a stand
Of Douglas fir, your legs straddled wide
Over the length of your penis,
Your back arched over generations,
Your narrow jaw grinding sideways,
Ears flopping sideways, your eyes
Big as moons in opposition
As you tear the green
Grass at its roots.

And here by the fence,
Just a few feet away,
You toss your white head,
Which is the colour of those who remember
    nothing,
And the massive horns curl out and around

At commotions in the air.
But you have no fear, knowing
Here there are no heads to butt with:
You are the unchallenged king
Of a harem of ewes, eating
And catching your breath,
Though your mind, like a weather-beaten road
Is always falling into the ditches.

Still, it is here, well-protected,
That you stand rivetted
Like the thicket-snared ram
That dies instead of the son,
Dying like a constellation
That frames a small part of the dark
Some get over, the dark you are doomed to die
    in.

# ARCTIC WOLF

*(Canis arcticus)*

The light in your eyes still shines
Though your antics are reduced
To those of the common dog. You even live
In a doghouse in a grove
Behind a tall chain-link fence.
Except for your eyes,
You do not look fierce at all,
Propped scarcely erect on skinny forelegs
In the dust, in the glare, of a hot day.
What you are now is the small grey-white hunter
At the edge of the shimmering vista of emptiness
Broken by the shade and seeming too permanent
To be any day the afternoon. Yet you see into it,
The distance that shines and waves and weighs.
But you do not have at all the air of vigilance,
And you stand by the fence shrunken in the
    puddle
Of your shadow. From your mouth
The pink tongue is faded. I do not beware you
As a ferocious dog but as a being harmless,
All glory lost, your wildness gone as a war
Against the fence, and though you be fed,
You are weak—though you can see
Into us and through us free and untethered.
Surely, you would not attack, nor move
Except, perhaps, startled, to flee;

Surely, your unkempt coat could not rise
Hostile in hackles; and surely,
You would wish to growl. If you should
Bare your teeth with their fangs,
Who would notice the falling of the jaw
As it is with the grins of the dead?
Aside from the keeper who comes with food,
What might you look forward to? The leaves
	falling
Or the empty distance, your glazed eyes
Staring beyond us noticing nothing;
You do not see us but through us,
And the danger of your eyes is that in them
We are not here. But there is no fierceness
Left in you; you stand sentinel over a past
That no longer is. Your watch is endless.
Staring like a guard dog, you guard all that is
	gone,
And turning to leave, as we do, your tail
Down between your legs still guards
Your most delicate parts
And the distance between and beyond.

# ORANGUTAN

*(Simia satyrus)*


Ancestor,
Subject of our dark *études*, you jump
Up screaming and rattle
The door of your cage, hands
And feet gripping the metal bars:
Then comes the dashing from wall to wall
And the wedging of your head
Between the bars.

But the outburst is only temporary.
You lie down in the centre, the cage's heart,
Basking in sunlight like a drugged mental patient
In a violent ward, brown eyes watching
Left to right, right to left, the passers-by
Who laugh at their reflections in the glass.

Inside, around you, are bars to swing from
And the amputated limbs of small trees,
But there is no place to swing to,
No place but the concrete floor or the glass wall,
The first echoing the nothing of caged days,
The second mirroring the illusion of someone else
Who ends up being you alone.

Outside, the PLEASE DO NOT FEED sign
Is glued to the barred window,

And no one does, not even the children,
As the cage continues to keep
What's in in and what's out out
Like a second skin in which you are
The wound refusing to heal.
Bored and desperate and starving,
You pick a carrot up off the floor,
Grind it and gnaw it, covering your mouth
Like a strange Ugolino eating his hands.

GOLDFINCH

*(Spinus tristis)*


In your bright plumage
                    You are
                    The sun that blazes
In a dark cage of glass

                    One hears
                    A flute concerto
                    In a closed space
                    Play the silences
                    As well as the notes

You preen the feathers around your heart

Even here
          Song is an inner journey
          Between invisible distances

Yet you leap from the branch into fetid air
          And with surprising speed
Collide
          A brief thud
                    Against the window
Breaking your neck to get out

# THE OCTOPUS OF EITHER/OR/OR

*(Octopus vulgaris)*

*Vancouver Aquarium*


Like a fossil suddenly liberated
From a dark rock,
You hide visibly in stillness
At the bottom of the tank
Of circulating sea water.

Medusa's severed head
Petrifying in death as in life,
You are locked in a compass of arms
That strike like snakes
Surrounding
The crawling crab
Whose exoskeleton
Cracks open in your beak
Revealing the targeted heart.

Your monstrosity is, however, a beauty
The beautifies like death,
Your ontology that of a heart gone bad
After learning the ways of the sea
Only to freeze in fear at your own
Reflected face in the glass.

Or

Orpheus' head
Still singing of the ocean's depths
In sea creatures
Gathered at the bottom.

Crustaceans listen and wonder
At the tide of your song
Pulling in them like a magnet
And flowing through them like a current

Whose vacancy you fill
With the places you have been
Mercurial as meaning, the self
Finding self
In a cloud of ink.

Or

In the cluttered light of the tank,
You are clearly *octopoda*,
A cephalopod that thrives
On maintaining
Its hold on others
In the dark.

# RAINBOW TROUT

*(Salmo shasta)*

*Vancouver Aquarium*

Prismed light shines darker
Like a great melancholy
Becalmed in a glass tank.

Though you fin the water,
Twist in the artificial current
And swish your tail,
You are the same footprint
Many times over
In the circulating stream.

Always fighting the water,
You grow larger; always
Baring your trembling light,
You become a remembrance in memory

Like those in life
Who stay forever in the womb.

# ACROSTIC NUMBERS OF THE KILLER WHALE

*(Orcinus orca)*

*Vancouver Aquarium*

I.

In this precipitate of the ocean
The salmon's journey ends in an orange bucket,
And you heel balancing on flukes, shrieking,
The thorns of your teeth
Boring the white jaw to the jet.
But your heart is firm as steel,
As hard as it is human:
You whip the pool to foam and boil,
Stir the water against itself,
For while you are open, the waters closed,
Steam and salt spray spout behind you
Like smoke from a locomotive.

II.

Yet of supplications from you we have many,
Even before the volcano of you rises
In opposing hues from this blue
To touch the red ball high at the end
Of a long baton. For a hungry stomach
Must do tricks, though your blow hole singing
Like a fontanelle breathes all into singing,

And your sigh in this curt shallow
Is only of a remembered depth.

III.

Magpie of the waters, we play with you,
And although the pink flame
Of your tongue be not split,
We talk in play and our play is talk.
But you, in the silent deep
Of a greater matter speak,
And many there are who
In your hard breach find delight,
Though frightened by your whirling
Of the pool to cresting waves
And the full and burning
Millstone of your heart.

IV.

Oh, that you were not fooled
By the stroking hand
On the fist of your forehead
Or the captured harems
Passing through your passing pleasure.
Not one of you born here lives on
But is abortion
To the sterile ghost of the place.

V.

While no fear in us of you
Be betrayed, who would anger
Or play you out of meekness
Becomes the toy and drowns
In this integument of water
Amid confused applause.

VI.

As we sit frivolous beside the still waters
You inhabit, you are an island unto yourself.
Seen from below, you are floating
Drift ice, the mottled berg
Of this dwarfed sea, a whiteness
Extending farther than I can see;
From above, you are blacker than the black
Ocean depths or any mine
Where no light reaches.
But the lantern of your face and fire
Awakens the blind and halcyon dead;
And from all sides, you are the onyx
And starry pupil
In this pool's blue eye.

VII.

Though you bask in light, floating,
Your eyes like the moons of Mars are
In opposition juxtaposed,

To one gravity committed,
As lovers leaning in no distance
In one face. Thus you grow
To ply the waters like a rolling hill,
And in your leaping jump at stars
Find altitude enough
For that knotted forehead to unfurl,
To drink whole clouds, to furl,
To pound, side bellowing,
The closed sea into waves
That overflow their shores, or
As here, splash off the walls
Of shrunken dominion.

# V.
# SOLILOQUIES
# OF
# THE
# STATUES

# LORD STANLEY

For peace of mind I became hard,
Quiet where whispers announce me,
I who had longed to be immune
To idle tongues that infest the air.

I chastened the body where it dreamed,
I hushed all offices till I
Quiet and blind as Justice seem,
And I reign in a still kingdom.

I banished motion, but have found
No simplicity in bronze,
For those who come believe and bend
Before me and make me many things.

Both cause and image I became,
The innocent who grieves,
The condemned who would boast,
Yet I of both the mirror am.

I am the patience of a pool
Where all the planets sway, and I
Am the moon's self, a watery star
Beheld at night near Lost Lagoon.

I am the night where all are blind,
And I, the orbit of their prayers;
Quiet above the suppliant hand,

I am the heaven of fixed stars.

And I the elusive Phoenix seem,
And a man is my age and fire,
For the sculptor has breathed me to this flame,
And I, seeming myself, seem fire.

Thus I who have not moved a limb,
Who feigned but changelessness and keep
Only the semblance that I was,
Am the still point in revolving time.

## HARRY JEROME

Why I am running the sculptor knew—
If I am running. Or if it is only the wind,
A wind risen along the slope of the shore,
Suddenly, as a fish leaps, lifting my garments,
My feet like music, a whirling of breath
Melted here to solidify in a narrow place
That is enough for a man. If only you could see
The wind in my gait, but in itself not,
You could hear a spirit in its motion,
In its words, even in its stillness,
But not in itself. Know it here
In the stance of a runner
And in his head arched against the sky
As in an archway; know it in the dust
That is deaf, for even stones
Can rise with feet when my spirit passes
Upon the place where they are,
Even though they have grown backward.
There is no measure nor soundness
In them when I pass. My legs are strong,
Making the music they move to:
Light like fire. They shall be moved
With burning this wind moves not,
Though I bare down and am with it always.
And yet, will the wind of heaven
Wear the shape of a man,
Be mortal as breath for a sign and stand
Between win or loss,

The thieves of the left and right hands?
So there is terrible gentleness
Unleashed in the bronze of my eyes;
So the wind runs as a fire,
As a starting pistol,
As the mountains leap, swelling,
As my feet, and I faithful upon them,
Leap always into
The stride that is all strides.

# THE SHAKESPEARE MEMORIAL

Observe not the bas relief
Of my image in a brick wall,
But the garden, for I am
Where birdsong, melodious, greets the ear,
Where all ranks, conditions and degrees
Of growth are in fact the phoenix
That lives in the rising
And falling of the plants,
In the budding and falling of the leaves.
Notice how the bees pollinating seize
And set free the honeyed flowers;
Notice the butterflies with idle effort
Plundering one by one the nectaries
Of deepest-throated blooms;
Notice the path lined with cherry trees
In white blossom, that leads through an arbour
To the forest, and on it two lovers
Returning to embrace and watch black squirrels
Dance on the newly-mown lawn.
Everywhere, see me in the bronze notes
Of the sun's great harp
As it strikes the trees into song.

# WOMAN ON A PARK BENCH

Here on the edge of green I sit
Alone and seeming the sculptor's design,
A life-sized bronze surrounding
A hollow core where once beat a heart,
Where now throbs a friendly darkness
Rubbing itself into a song
Only my ears hear:
The song of silence after love.

Yet I am deaf and do not hear
The traffic screech and halt,
Nor passers-by say I look real.
I am real, though I appear dead to them
And hear them all with the ears of the dead.
And I do not smell the flowers or taste blood;
Do not see the children sitting beside me
As they poke my dress with gaming fingers
Or fumble my breasts till they are
The only part of me that shines.
Nor do I feel the warm breeze grow cold.

A thing once living, a model, I am
Only the semblance of what I was.
Given the likeness of life,
I cannot move but am moving:
I am as a creature locked
In the compass of a cage
Wherein the four winds converge

But do not blow; given form
I cannot turn but am turning
Like a compass needle
Where love is the only true north;
Given movement of line, I cannot bend,
But am bending over, as you see,
Alone and untouched by tenderness.

Behold what has become of me,
I who waited for love still wait and wait forever
Beyond my cool integument,
Locked in a pose of sitting
In all weathers intent
Upon my bronze purse, in which it seems
I have lost everything.
Touch me now. Unsculpt the sculpted dark,
And know the loneliness of a statue
Is the loneliness of a woman,
Is the loneliness of the world.

# GIRL IN A WETSUIT

As if I had been swimming and seen all,
I rest myself on a barnacled rock
In a ray of light, my flippers still
On my feet, a skin diver becalmed,
Rendered immoveable by nothing,
By everything I have seen of the sea.
And what I have seen are whole schools of fish
In their lessons swaying,
As if in the tide's influence,
Attacked and eaten by larger fish
Until only the largest looming
Inherit the tide's hungry sway.
And I have seen sharks scavenge
What's left after the slaughter,
Even the guts and scales
That lived in the light they thought was theirs.
And I have seen octopuses clinging
To the rocky depths, their arms
Shuttling across the sea floor
Trying to embrace me on the bottom.
I have seen everything eating everything else,
And everything, once eaten, is forgotten,
Not even a memory of what they were.
But what I see now, now that my mask
Is high on my forehead, is a harbour
Beset by enveloping piers that hug
The hulls of the whores of commerce,
Their poisonous cargoes turning me green

With the gull crap on my head,
Freezing me in time, an ornament here,
Yet prominent as a child in a shock of light
As if I were mistress of it all.

# THE HARDING MEMORIAL

The south and all that the south means,
I come like a lover, north,
President of the great republic,
To declare geographical embrace
In the shape of a wall.

But the longest undefended
Boarder in the world
Is the longest undefended boarder,
Is the world.

# THE JAPANESE WAR MEMORIAL

Nothing stentorian; nothing verbose.
Yet the names of the dead are many.
I stand above shining my light
Every day, every night,
Every season of the year,
Commemorating those who fell
To the Hun's guns and gas in France
As they stood guard for thee, O Canada.

These yellow platoons who were themselves
Their only light
Now mingle with the dust,
That great marcher in France,
Where nothing it comes to
Is alive for long.

These thought the living worth it,
No matter the mud and the blood,
And knew not only who they were
But the freedom they were fighting for
As rain fell into their opened eyes
Again and again with a pointless sound
Calling to nothing living.

When World War I was over,
We were proud enough. Still are
That the air over there
Is good enough for breathing at last,

95

That the silence of heaven migrates there
More perfectly, that here in Stanley Park
These plaques at my base
Form a new chessboard where a child in play
Dances the hopscotch of his own inner music
Over the names of the dead.

# THE CHEHALIS MONUMENT

This is what a small boat gives to tragedy:
A Celtic cross in a foreign land. Yet
None of us thought he would drown
With land so close. It was on both sides
Of us as we slowed in the straight. Yet
None of us could swim; all eight of us
Were lost. In the silence
After the first ramming, the crew's hearts
Were struck with a hollowness
That streamed up from the hull.
Then the bell rang telling us
It had been ringing, telling us
That it would strike home,
Hollow in the hearts of us. Only then
Did we hear it over the sunlight,
The dozing creak of the moorings,
The heat, the coiled lines
Asleep in their shadows,
And it sprang upon the light,
Bitter and heavy with sound.
And it was clear, in the middle of the straight
We were lost in a drifting dream
That had gone bad in a sea that was blind,
Wild and in a sudden rage,
Though calm as it seemed then.
And we were fairly sure where we were,
But the familiar waters fooled us
Into thinking there was no need

To be alarmed. There were waves, too,
But gentle, and the swell spared us.
Yet we died waiting
For someone to save us.

# VI.  OTHER VENUES

# THE HOLLOW TREE

What could have honed out
The rings around so huge a heart?
Dry rot, blight, a rust or mite
Invading the outside foliage,
Eating at the core of being?
A vertical wind would have sufficed.
Yet the sheer size of it,
The hollowness, the gaping hole
Where once its muscles were
Xylem and phloem
Are a great vacancy that attests
To the elements Nature musters
From within and without.

Whether inside or outside causes,
Both or neither,
This emptiness is now
The centre of gravity.

Shout into it,
And your voice does not echo,
But disappears in the hulk,
Never to return, like a love
Long after it has ended.

# SEAWALL

It meanders like a wet black eel
Along the shoreline of the park,
Avoiding its forested heart,
Holding it in like a breath,
Like a constricting noose,
But never completely, for even
The land rebels against it
In the northern reaches
Where rocks fall from cliffs
And pock the pavement with deep holes.

Clearly, there is danger here,
But at each turn there is a new sprawling vista
Of bays, the harbour, and the mountains.
In short, you can walk on it and laugh
At the plunging sea, but at high tide,
Waves splash over it, and you'll get wet,
If not knocked down and left gasping for air.
Still, some play games with the sea, thinking
They'll get through and be missed
By the crashing swells. But the sea
Misses no one and is everywhere,
Even this high above its shifting surface,
And certainly, it will take more
Than this wall to stop it.

Just the same, you can imagine
While pacing the five miles of its path

That you are walking on the sea itself,
Another determined Jesus,
So close are you to its surface.
And you do walk on it in the dream-like
Momentum of your pace
As bicyclists, roller-bladers, joggers
And strollers follow their lanes
Around the park's perimeter
Only to pass each other like strangers
Lost at sea.

# FOG

We no longer know where we are,
For this came up in the dark
While most of us slept. Still we awoke
Into it, rising from familiar dreams
Of ships at anchor in English Bay,
Of the orange and blue docks of the harbour,
Of the surrounding sea and mountains.
But none of that is visible,
And it is this blindness
That brings us down to earth.
For hours, now, it has been drifting
In no wind, as if it had a mind of its own.
We can only see a few feet ahead,
But we can hear the waves thudding.
Turning our heads, we pick up
The distant moan of the harbour horn
Sounding like a lowing cow, warning us
Of a storm we dare not ignore
Least we come upon one another
Too suddenly and crash, too late,
As our cries are swallowed up,
And no one survives. Still, everyone
Slows down in his or her course
But still seem adrift, like the blind,
And collide whether they look or don't.
And most don't. They yield to no one
They can see, and the cries from collisions
Rise up, but not for long. The fog

Swallows everything. Where are we?
Everyone else is a dark sceptre
In the distance, mere shadows up close.
In all this blinding grey
What have we to offer each other
But love in ignorance?

# NINE O'CLOCK GUN

Off it goes, like a bomb
Or a bird flying against a drum,
And the echo ricochets
Off buildings in the East End,
Where its muzzle is directed,
Awakening drunks lying asleep
On the sidewalk, interrupting
A lover's quarrel
Between two Natives,
Sending a cloudburst of pigeons
Into the air in Pigeon Park,
Punctuating the silence
With the cracking roar and gush
Of the broken wind.
A moment later, the drunks
Go back to sleep,
The lovers back to their argument,
And the pigeons back to their breadcrumbs
Until tomorrow night
At nine o'clock.

# COAL HARBOUR

Tranquility basin. A place
Like the mind's eye to set out from
Or be becalmed in as the south
Shoreline fills with glass towers
Scraping the sky.

Here too, in the blue air
The masts of the yachts
Nodding with the tide inscribe
Faint messages of what transpires
Below the creaking decks.

A few of us in perpetual winter
Repair our crafts in the blue slips,
Stoke more charcoal into our stoves,
Have dinner on tilting tables,
Spend the whole solstice in our hulls,
Waiting for the weather to break enough
To begin the great voyage out of the doldrums
Of space and mind, to round the bend
And enter the deceptively calm waters
Through the harbour and up the coast,
Or down, to find our way beyond
High winds and tempests
Only the craziest venture even now.

But there is some wisdom to their madness.
They say that a storm is the true test

Of a sailor, that knowing rough water,
Knowing the wind is knowing
How each breathes out of its hollow
Beyond the reckoning of instruments,
How each can demand more of rigging
And prow than what they're made of.
In the end, it is always the mettle
Of the mind, the fine-tuned timbre
Of thought that navigates the sea.
And yet, the best captain knows best
When to venture out, when to stay in port.

And most of us here have decided:
Better to wait, stay in the cove and be safe
From the squalls. Why test fate?

Occasionally, though, despite our warnings,
One of us will leave under auxiliary
In a hole in the weather, fooled by this place
Where the wind never reaches
And the water, though tidal, is a smooth mirror
To get lost in in reflecting
On the seemingly indomitable buoyancy
Of our craft and the dominant blue
Of the boat sheds, reflecting on
The odd heron fishing and finding nothing,
Reflecting that we are here becalmed
Come rain, come snow, reflecting on
The impossible voyage beyond what we know,
The one we will never take if we stay here.

# LIONS GATE BRIDGE

A green rainbow
Joining the concrete canyons
Of the North Shore
To the concrete canyons
Of the South:
Between its ends
A thriving commerce
Only a bridge allows.

Yet the old span is a poverty:
Light shines through its rusting cables
And pitted towers, daylight gapes
Through cracks in its road-bed,
And the great nuts and bolts together
Loose their threads and come undone.
You can hear the steel plates shift,
Clang and clatter like funeral bells
Tolling of the day when all traffic
Will fall through the cracks.

Clearly, it needs repair,
Like any green metaphor,
If anyone is to survive
The journey between shores,
A journey like all journeys
That beyond reaching
Through all the cold distance
Of endings, touches and connects.

## JUBILEE FOUNTAIN

The green and murky water
Of Lost Lagoon lies stagnant
And still as a corpse, but here
It is thrown up like a living mind
That, wind-honed, escapes gravity
And dances over our heads
Into the blue
Where it is resurrected,
A silver column of spray
That seems to hold up the sky.

All day and all night
The steady hiss of the jet
Rises and falls, falls and rises,
In pulsating stages as if alive,

But, at a certain height, it falls
Under its own weight,
Though it is far from heavy,
And floats, atomized by the wind
Into a fine mist of diamonds
Prismatic in the light,
Finding its primary colours
As it fills hollows in the air
And the space between us
Who, mostly water, walked out of it
Long ago.  Even now our eyes
Smart from the light,

And our ears are renewed with listening
As the spray touching down hisses once more
On the surface of Lost Lagoon.

# THIRD BEACH

The beach is small but full
Of children making in the twining tide
The motions of birds
Pursued by the surf.

And the blue ocean is a mirror
As waves break the rocks they break on,
As the wind over the water
Chops the light into pieces.

And the dull shore of the sand refrains
As the breakers crash like an old surf
Breaking far away in the blood of a man
As he watches his son build a sand castle.

Further on, a bathing child
Wades through his shadow in the water:
Though he trample and kick it, the sea
Recomposes, embracing the musculature of the
    shore.

# SIWASH ROCK

This is not the first time
A god turned a good man to stone.

After their hearts have been torn
Out of their chests,
Most rocks rising over the sea
Become cold, inflexible and mean
Living death like ravens
By stealth alone.

But this one stays put, taking
The waves that break at its feet
In a stride beginning and ending here
That is wedded to the earth.

# IN THE FOREST

On a map at the park entrance,
So many paths and trails
Like veins and arteries
Of the green heart
Tell where they lead to:
So many places to get lost.

Yet, there are destinations,
I find, as they find me,
All of them moving as I move
As I keep walking through the wild
Labyrinth of crossroads
And *cul de sacs*, knowing
The way has been paved
With black-top like a warning
Warning me not to go overland,
Warning of the heart of darkness
Those who have gone before me
Have found like their own.

But left or right on the path,
The forest is still. The tallest
Stands of ancient trees are few
But lead to the deepest dark,
And secondary growth, almost topiary,
Predominates, the evergreens
Keeping their counsel,

Finding the way out of their own dark
By maintaining a safe distance.

Straight ahead, the hardwood leaves
Finding their voices
Have learned how to fly
Till they fall on their shadows,

And around me, here at the heart
Of the heart of the forest, pale seedlings
Sprout from deadfalls called nurse logs,
Cowering at the understorey
As the green canopy blots out the sky
From a love of light.

Everywhere I go now I ignore
The emptiness at the heart of light,
The fullness at the heart of darkness.
Though I have walked blind through it
All of my life, this is the garden
I keep coming back to
Where everything is strangely familiar.

# ABOUT THE AUTHOR

R. W. STEDINGH was born in Camden, New Jersey in 1944. He was educated at Glassboro State College (now Rowan University) and Rutger's University, and from 1966 to 1968, he worked as an English teacher in Swiss private schools. Since then he has become a Canadian citizen, received an M. A. in Creative Writing from the University of British Columbia and started post-graduate work in Comparative Literature at the University of Toronto. From 1970 to 1971 he was Managing Editor of *PRISM international* and from 1970 to 1974, the Founding Editor of the *Canadian Fiction Magazine*. His poetry, fiction and translations from the French, Spanish and Estonian have appeared widely in the English-speaking world. He is the author of three books of poetry, *Faces of Eve, From a Bell Tower* and *The Stanley Park Suite*. He is also the translator (with T. E. Moks) of *Arved Viirlaid: Selected Poems*, which is scheduled for publication next year. He lives in Vancouver.